1949 A Time Travel's Guide: Flashback Se

In the Embrac
A Journey Through Time

Celebrating your year
1949
A memorable year for

TABLE OF CONTENTS

INTRODUCTION

1. POLITIC
Remarkable political events of '49.................. 7
Major World Political Leaders in 1949.......... 14
Activity: Historical Trivia Quiz Test Your Knowledge of 1949.. 18

2. ENTERTAINMENT
Films and Prestigious Film Awards................ 22
Music: Top Songs and Awards....................... 29
Activity: Let's guess the the name of song from the lyrics... 39

3. ART AND LITERATURE
Popular books published............................... 41
Arts in 1949.. 45
Activity: Search puzzle related to Literature and Art in 1949.. 55

4. SPORTS
Sport Winner and Awards............................... 54
Activity: Test Your Knowledge of 1949 Sports History... 61

5. FASHION, AND POPULAR LEISURE ACTIVITIES
Fashion... 65
Popular Leisure Activities.............................. 70
Activity: Let's draw a picture of the "fashion of 1949"... 71

TABLE OF CONTENTS

TECHNOLOGY AND INNOVATION
Technological events 73
The Automobiles of 1949 77
Activity: Test Your Knowledge of Technology
in 1949 82

THE COST OF THINGS
The Cost of Things 84
Activity: How the life changed 87

BIRTHS IN 1949
Notable individuals were born 89
Activity: "Profiles in Achievement: The Noteworthy
Births of 1949" 99

Special gift for readers 103
Activity answers 104

Introduction

"Journeying through 1949: A Heartfelt Tribute to a Timeless Era"

Step into the captivating world of 1949, where each page tells a story of hope, resilience, and the unwavering spirit of a generation. Whether you experienced the wonders of this year firsthand or inherited its legacy from cherished tales, this book is a heartfelt ode to the lasting echoes of an unforgettable time.

Come along as we unravel the rich tapestry of 1949, a year that left an indelible mark on the annals of history. Through a collection of heartwarming narratives, cultural snapshots, and cherished memories, we invite you to rediscover the magic and nostalgia woven into the fabric of this extraordinary chapter.

With each turn of the page, may you find comfort, inspiration, and a renewed sense of connection to the vibrant stories that continue to shape our world. Join us on this journey through 1949, where the past comes alive, and the spirit of an era whispers its timeless tales.

Warmest regards,
Edward Art Lab

Chapter 1: World Politics

In 1949, the world was still in the process of recovering from the aftermath of World War II, and the political landscape was significantly shaped by the emerging tensions of the Cold War. Some key events and developments in world politics during 1949:

1. Remarkable political events of '49
The end of the Berlin Blockade

- The Berlin Blockade was a major crisis of the early Cold War. It began in 1948 when the Soviet Union, which controlled East Germany, blocked all land and water access to the western-controlled sectors of Berlin, effectively cutting off West Berlin from the outside world.
- The blockade lasted for nearly a year and led to the Berlin Airlift, in which Western Allied forces supplied West Berlin with food, fuel, and other necessities by air.
- The blockade officially ended on May 12, 1949, when the Soviets lifted the blockade. This event marked a significant moment in the early tensions of the Cold War.

The proclamation of the Communist People's Republic of China

On October 1, 1949, Mao Zedong officially declared the establishment of the People's Republic of China, marking the end of a long period of civil war and the beginning of a new era for China. The establishment of the Communist government under Mao's leadership had far-reaching consequences for China's domestic and international policies. It also significantly impacted global geopolitics during the Cold War.

The formation of NATO

On April 4, 1949, NATO (North Atlantic Treaty Organization) was created as a military alliance of Western countries in response to the perceived threat of the Soviet Union during the early years of the Cold War.'

Formation of the Council of Europe

The Council of Europe is an international organization founded in 1949 to promote greater unity and cooperation among European countries, particularly in the areas of human rights, democracy, and the rule of law. The key objectives of the Council of Europe include: *democracy, human rights and the rule of law.*

The recognition of Indonesian independence by the Netherlands

The Dutch-Indonesian Round Table Conference, which took place from August 23 to November 2, 1949, was a significant diplomatic event that marked the trans-!fer of sovereignty of the Dutch East Indies to the Republic of Indonesia. The negotiations at the conference resulted in the recognition of Indonesian independence by the Netherlands, thereby ending the Indonesian National Revolution, a period of armed and diplomatic resistance against Dutch colonial rule.

The signing of the Geneva Conventions on August 12, 1949

The signing of the Geneva Conventions on August 12, 1949, marked a significant development in the field of international humanitarian law. The conventions were a set o-f four treaties that established the standards for the humane treatment of individuals during armed conflicts, including the protection of civilians, wounded soldiers, and prisoners of war.

The four Geneva Conventions of 1949 were:
- *Geneva Convention for the Amelioration of the Condition of the Wounded and Sick in Armed Forces in the Field.*
- *Geneva Convention for the Amelioration of the Condition of Wounded, Sick, and Shipwrecked Members of Armed Forces at Sea.*
- *Geneva Convention relative to the Treatment of Prisoners of War.*
- *Geneva Convention relative to the Protection of Civilian Persons in Time of War.*

These conventions laid the groundwork for the establishment of crucial international laws and principles that aimed to mitigate the suffering of individuals affected by armed conflicts and to protect their basic rights.

The Geneva Conventions continue to serve as fundamental instruments for the protection of human dignity during times of war and armed conflict.

2. Major World Political Leaders in 1949

Harry S. Truman

Harry S. Truman, as the President of the United States, played a pivotal role in shaping American foreign policy during the early years of the Cold War. His presidency was marked by the implementation of the Truman Doctrine and the Marshall Plan, which aimed to contain the spread of communism and support the economic recovery of war-torn Europe.

Clement Attlee

Clement Attlee, as the Prime Minister of the United Kingdom, played a significant role in the post-war reconstruction of Britain. His administration focused on rebuilding the British economy, implementing social welfare reforms, and overseeing the process of decolonization.

Konrad Adenauer

Konrad Adenauer played a crucial role as the Chancellor of Germany, overseeing the reconstruction and reintegration of West Germany into the global community. His policies focused on economic recovery and fostering stronger ties with Western allies.

Jawaharlal Nehru

Jawaharlal Nehru, as the Prime Minister of India, played a crucial role in shaping the country's foreign policy and domestic development. He advocated for non-alignment during the Cold War and championed the principles of democracy and secularism.

Mao Zedong

Mao Zedong, as the Chairman of the People's Republic of China, led the nation through a period of significant social and political transformation. His leadership was instrumental in the establishment of the People's Republic of China and the implementation of various policies aimed at reshaping China's political and social structures.

Joseph Stalin

Joseph Stalin, as the Chairman of the Council of People's Commissars of the Soviet Union, continued to exert strong influence over the Soviet Union's political and social policies. His leadership was marked by the further consolidation of Soviet power and the propagation of communist ideologies across Eastern Europe.

Alcide De Gasperi

Alcide De Gasperi, as the Prime Minister of Italy, focused on rebuilding the country's economy and fostering stability in the aftermath of World War II. His leadership was instrumental in the formation of the Italian Republic and the subsequent economic recovery.

Shigeru Yoshida

Shigeru Yoshida, as the Prime Minister of Japan, oversaw the post-war reconstruction and democratization of the country. His administration worked towards rebuilding the Japanese economy and establishing strong diplomatic relations with the international community.

Activity: Historical Triava Quiz
Test Your Knowledge of 1949

Are you ready to challenge your knowledge of the significant events and key figures of 1949? Here's a historical trivia quiz to test your knowledge of the events and leaders in 1949:

1. Which international organization, focused on promoting human rights and democracy, was founded in 1949?
a) United Nations
b) European Union
c) NATO
d) Council of Europe

2. Who was the Chairman of the People's Republic of China in 1949, following the establishment of the People's Republic of China?
a) Chiang Kai-shek
b) Sun Yat-sen
c) Mao Zedong
d) Zhou Enlai

3. Which political figure served as the Prime Minister of India in 1949, advocating for non-alignment during the Cold War?
a) Mahatma Gandhi
b) Jawaharlal Nehru
c) Indira Gandhi
d) Rajendra Prasad

4. Who was the Chairman of the Council of People's Commissars in the Soviet Union in 1949, consolidating Soviet power in Eastern Europe?
a) Vladimir Lenin
b) Joseph Stalin
c) Nikita Khrushchev
d) Leon Trotsky

5. Who was the President of the United States in 1949, implementing the Truman Doctrine and the Marshall Plan?
a) Dwight D. Eisenhower
b) Franklin D. Roosevelt
c) Harry S. Truman
d) John F. Kennedy

6. Which political leader served as the Prime Minister of Japan in 1949, overseeing the post-war reconstruction and democratization of the country?
a) Hirohito
b) Shigeru Yoshida
c) Hideki Tojo
d) Eisaku Sato

7.What was the primary purpose of NATO when it was founded?
a) Economic cooperation
b) Military alliance against the Soviet Union
c) Humanitarian aid
d) Cultural exchange

8. Which prominent political figure was the Prime Minister of Italy in 1949, leading the country's economic recovery and stability after World War II?
a) Benito Mussolini
b) Alcide De Gasperi
c) Giuseppe Garibaldi
d) Silvio Berlusconi

Chapter 2: Entertainment in 1949

Entertainment in 1949 was marked by a resurgence of optimism and revitalization after the tumultuous years of World War II.

Films and Prestigious Film Awards

1. Memorable Films of '49
"All the King's Men"- Robert Rossen

"All the King's Men" is a political drama film directed by Robert Rossen. It is based on the Pulitzer Prize-winning novel of the same name by Robert Penn Warren. The film's portrayal of the rise and fall of a corrupt politician earned critical acclaim, and it won the Academy Award for Best Picture in 1949.

"The Third Man"- Carol Reed

"The Third Man," directed by Carol Reed, is widely recognized as a cinematic masterpiece that garnered critical acclaim for its atmospheric portrayal of post-war Vienna. Released in 1949, the film is known for its exceptional use of shadowy cinematography and its innovative storytelling techniques, which contributed to its enduring legacy in the film noir genre.

"On the Town"- Stanley Donen & Gene Kelly

"On the Town," directed by Stanley Donen and Gene Kelly, is a beloved musical film that showcases the adventures of three sailors during a 24-hour shore leave in New York City. The film is known for its vibrant and energetic portrayal of the city, as well as its lively musical numbers and memorable songs, including the iconic anthem "New York, New York."

"On the Town" captures the excitement and spirit of New York City and became a favorite among audiences.

"Battleground"- William A

"Battleground" is a 1949 American war film directed by William A. Wellman. The movie was well-received by audiences and critics for its honest portrayal of the human side of war, and it remains a notable entry in the genre of World War II films.

"White Heat"- Raoul Walsh

""White Heat," released in 1949, remains one of the most influential crime films of its time, leaving a lasting impact on the film noir genre and popular culture. This film has endured as a timeless classic that continues to inspire filmmakers and entertain audiences with its compelling storytelling and powerful performances.

2. Prestigious Film Awards

The 21st Academy Awards were held on March 24, 1949, honoring film industry for the year 1938. Here is the breakdown of the awards:

Academy Awards (Oscars)

Best Picture & Best Actor
Laurence Olivier for "Hamlet"

Best Director & Best Screenplay
John Huston for The Treasure of the Sierra Madre

Best Actress:
Jane Wyman for "Johnny Belinda"

Best Supporting Actor:
Walter Huston for
"The Treasure of the Sierra Madre

Best Supporting Actress
Claire Trevor – Key Largo

Best Motion Picture Story:
Richard Schweizer for "The Search"

3. The TV show The Goldbergs

One of the first long-running and successful sitcoms, "The Goldbergs," first aired live on CBS on January 17, 1949. The sitcom revolved around the daily lives of a Jewish family in New York City, delving into the ordinary struggles and triumphs of their daily existence. "The Goldbergs" addressed the challenges of maintaining cultural identity while assimilating into American society, tackling issues that resonated with a diverse audience. "The Goldbergs" remained on the air until 1956, leaving a lasting legacy in the history of American television.

Music: Top Songs and Awards

1. Top songs

Here are some significant musical highlights from that year

Riders in the Sky- Vaughn Monroe

"Riders in the Sky" was indeed a hit for Vaughn Monroe. The song, released in 1949, was based on the American cowboy song that goes by the same name. Vaughn Monroe's version was a popular rendition and helped popularize the song further. "Riders in the Sky" has since become a classic in the Western music genre and has been covered by numerous artists over the years.

Some Enchanted Evening

"Some Enchanted Evening" is a classic song from the musical "South Pacific" with music by Richard Rodgers and lyrics by Oscar Hammerstein II. While Perry Como is a renowned artist, his rendition of "Some Enchanted Evening" wasn't the most popular or iconic version of the song. However, his interpretation remains a notable one, showcasing his smooth and mellow vocal style. The song has become a timeless classic in the American songbook, known for its romantic and evocative lyrics.

You're Breaking My Heart

"You're Breaking My Heart" is a popular song that was recorded by Vic Damone. The song, with music by Pat Genaro and lyrics by Sunny Skylar, was released in 1949. Vic Damone's rendition of the song became a significant hit and one of his signature tracks.

That Lucky Old Sun

"That Lucky Old Sun" is a popular song that was recorded by Frankie Laine. Released in 1949, the song has since become one of his signature pieces.

Slippin' Around

"Slippin' Around" is a classic country and western duet performed by Jimmy Wakely and Margaret Whiting. The song, released in 1949, became a significant hit, reaching the top of the country music charts. The duet's harmonious blend and the heartfelt delivery of the lyrics contributed to the song's success and popularity. "Slippin' Around" remains a memorableg piece within the genre, known for its emotional resonance and expressive storytelling.

I Can Dream, Can't I

"I Can Dream, Can't I?" is a popular song recorded by the Andrews Sisters and Gordon Jenkins. Released in 1949, the song became a hit and is considered one of the notable tracks in the Andrews Sisters' repertoire. The song's wistful and romantic lyrics, combined with the Andrews Sisters' harmonious vocals and Gordon Jenkins' orchestration, contributed to its enduring appeal. "I Can Dream, Can't I?" remains a classic example of the music from that era, evoking a sense of longing and hopefulness.

2. Renowned Musicians and Bands of '49

In 1949, the music scene was alive with the sounds of renowned musicians and bands who made their mark on the era. Some of the notable figures and groups that captured the hearts of music enthusiasts in '49:

Frank Sinatra

Frank Sinatra was indeed a prominent figure in the music industry. Sinatra's influence continues to resonate with audiences, and his legacy as one of the greatest entertainers of the 20th century remains unparalleled.

Ella Fitzgerald

Often referred to as the "First Lady of Song" and the "Queen of Jazz," Fitzgerald made an indelible mark on the world of music with her unparalleled talent and versatility. In 1949, Fitzgerald's contributions to the world of jazz and popular music were widely celebrated, and her recordings continued to captivate audiences worldwide. Her distinctive voice and unparalleled musicality made her a standout artist, and her influence on the jazz genre during this period was profound and enduring.

Louis Armstrong

In 1949, Louis Armstrong was already a prominent and influential figure in the world of jazz music. As a pioneering jazz trumpeter and vocalist, Armstrong had already left an indelible mark on the development of jazz during the preceding decades.

Nat King Cole

Nat King Cole was indeed a celebrated musician known for his smooth baritone voice and significant contributions to jazz and popular music. By 1949, Cole had already established himself as a prominent figure in the music industry, gaining recognition for his rich vocal tone, impeccable phrasing, and elegant style.

Woody Herman and His Orchestra

Woody Herman and His Orchestra were indeed a well-known and highly regarded big band that made significant contributions to the world of jazz during 1949. Led by the renowned clarinetist and bandleader Woody Herman, the orchestra gained widespread recognition for their dynamic and energetic performances, as well as their innovative arrangements and compositions.

The Andrews Sisters:

In 1949, The Andrews Sisters, a popular vocal trio, were still a significant presence in the music industry. One of their notable song from 1949 included popular hit such as "I Can Dream, Can't I?"

Billie Holiday

In 1949, Billie Holiday, with her distinct vocal style and poignant interpretations, continued to be a celebrated and influential figure in the world of jazz and blues. Holiday released several notable recordings in 1949, showcasing her unique vocal phrasing and evocative storytelling. Renowned for her emotional depth and ability to infuse songs with raw, heartfelt emotion, Holiday's impact on the music industry during this time was profound.

Activity: Let's guess name of song from the lyrics

1. "An old cowpoke went riding out one dark and windy day..."
....

2. "Some enchanted evening, you may see a stranger, you may see a stranger across a crowded room..."
....

3. "Up in the mornin', out on the job, work like the devil for my pay..."
....

4. "I can see, no matter how near you'll be, you'll never belong to me...
....

Chapter 3: Art and Literature in 1949

In 1949, the world of art and literature experienced a vibrant and dynamic period with the emergence of various significant works and movements.

Popular books published in 1949

1. Nineteen Eighty-Four

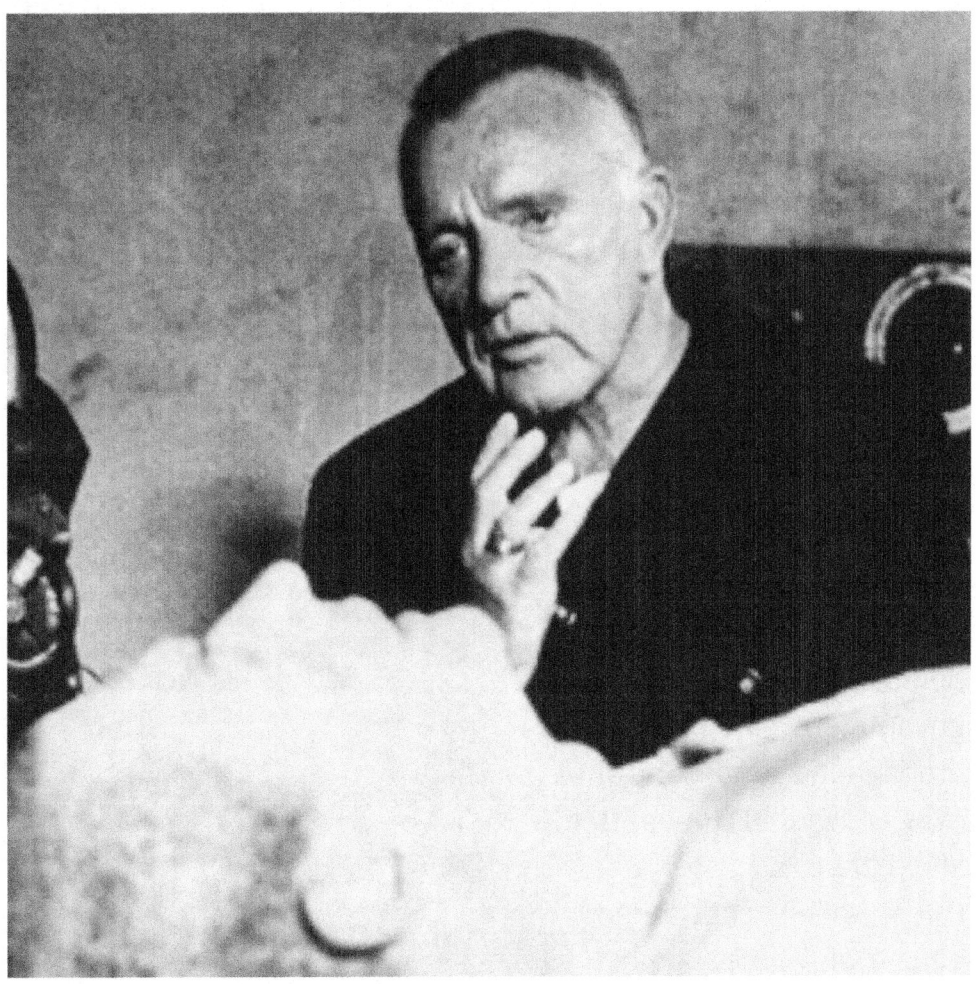

Published in 1949, the novel presents a bleak vision of a future world dominated by oppressive government surveillance, propaganda, and control over individual thoughts and actions.
It has been considered one of the most influential and enduring works of dystopian literature in the 20th century.

2. The Intelligent Investor

"The Intelligent Investor" is a renowned book on value investing, written by Benjamin Graham, a well-known economist and professional investor. First published in 1949, the book has become a classic in the world of finance and investment

3. Death of a Salesman

Published in 1949, the novel presents a bleak vision of a future world dominated by oppressive government surveillance, propaganda, and control over individual thoughts and actions.

It has been considered one of the most influential and enduring works of dystopian literature in the 20th century.

4. The Second Sex

"The Second Sex" is a pioneering work of feminist philosophy written by Simone de Beauvoir. First published in 1949, the book is considered an important milestone in the development of feminist philosophy and literature. "The Second Sex" remains a significant and enduring contribution to the ongoing conversation surrounding gender equality and women's rights.

5. The Hero With a Thousand Faces

"The Hero with a Thousand Faces" is a seminal work of comparative mythology written by Joseph Campbell. First published in 1949, the book explores the common themes and - archetypes found in world mythologies, folklore, and religious narratives. It celebrated for its insightful exploration of the human experience and its enduring impact on the study of mythology and narrative.T

Arts in 1949

In the realm of art, the year 1949 marked a period of diverse artistic movements and notable developments. Some of the significant artistic events and trends in 1949 included:

1. **Abstract Expressionism**: This art movement gained momentum, with prominent artists such as Jackson Pollock, Willem de Kooning, and Mark Rothko producing influential works that emphasized spontaneity, emotion, and gestural brushstrokes.
2. **Pablo Picasso:** The renowned Spanish artist continued to produce significant works, showcasing his evolving style and innovative approach to painting, sculpture, and ceramics.
3. **Surrealism**: Although past its peak, the Surrealist movement still had a notable presence, with artists such as Salvador Dalí and René Magritte producing thought-provoking and dreamlike artworks that challenged conventional perceptions of reality.
4. **European Art:** Post-war Europe saw a resurgence in artistic creativity, with artists exploring new forms of expression and experimenting with various styles and techniques in response to the socio-political climate of the time.

The 1949 Archibald Prize.

Arthur Murch's win with his portrait of Bonar Dunlop in 1949 contributed to the rich history and legacy of the Archibald Prize as one of the most esteemed art awards in Australia.

Bonar Dunlop oil
Winner of the Archibald Prize 1949

Arts

Jackson Pollock in 1949

Arts

The Madonna of Port Lligat

Arts

Two Dancers

Arts

The Fisherman's Return of Brenda Chamberlain

Arts

- *The Temple by Paul Delvaux*

Activity: Search puzzle related to Literature and Art in 1949

E	L	J	A	A	R	W	T	O	O	U	J	B	T
S	M	O	A	T	T	C	R	S	P	H	E	W
M	L	S	R	A	B	A	P	R	S	E	T	N	O
S	I	E	T	H	P	H	U	L	A	U	H	J	D
I	T	P	H	N	J	M	M	A	C	R	E	A	A
L	E	H	U	S	O	L	G	H	I	O	S	M	N
A	R	C	R	E	O	V	M	E	P	P	E	I	C
E	A	A	M	S	T	S	E	R	O	E	C	N	E
R	T	M	U	G	I	E	E	L	L	A	O	G	R
R	U	P	R	E	E	E	R	P	B	N	N	R	S
U	R	B	C	T	H	H	O	H	A	A	D	A	E
S	E	E	H	R	E	T	J	A	P	R	S	H	H
A	E	L	P	M	E	T	E	H	T	T	E	A	L
I	B	L	O	C	E	H	U	P	O	E	X	M	N

THE TEMPLE
JOSEPH CAMPBELL
THE SECOND SEX
TWO DANCERS
PABLO PICASSO

BENJAMIN GRAHAM
NOVEL
SURREALISM
EUROPEAN ART
ARTHUR MURCH
LITERATURE

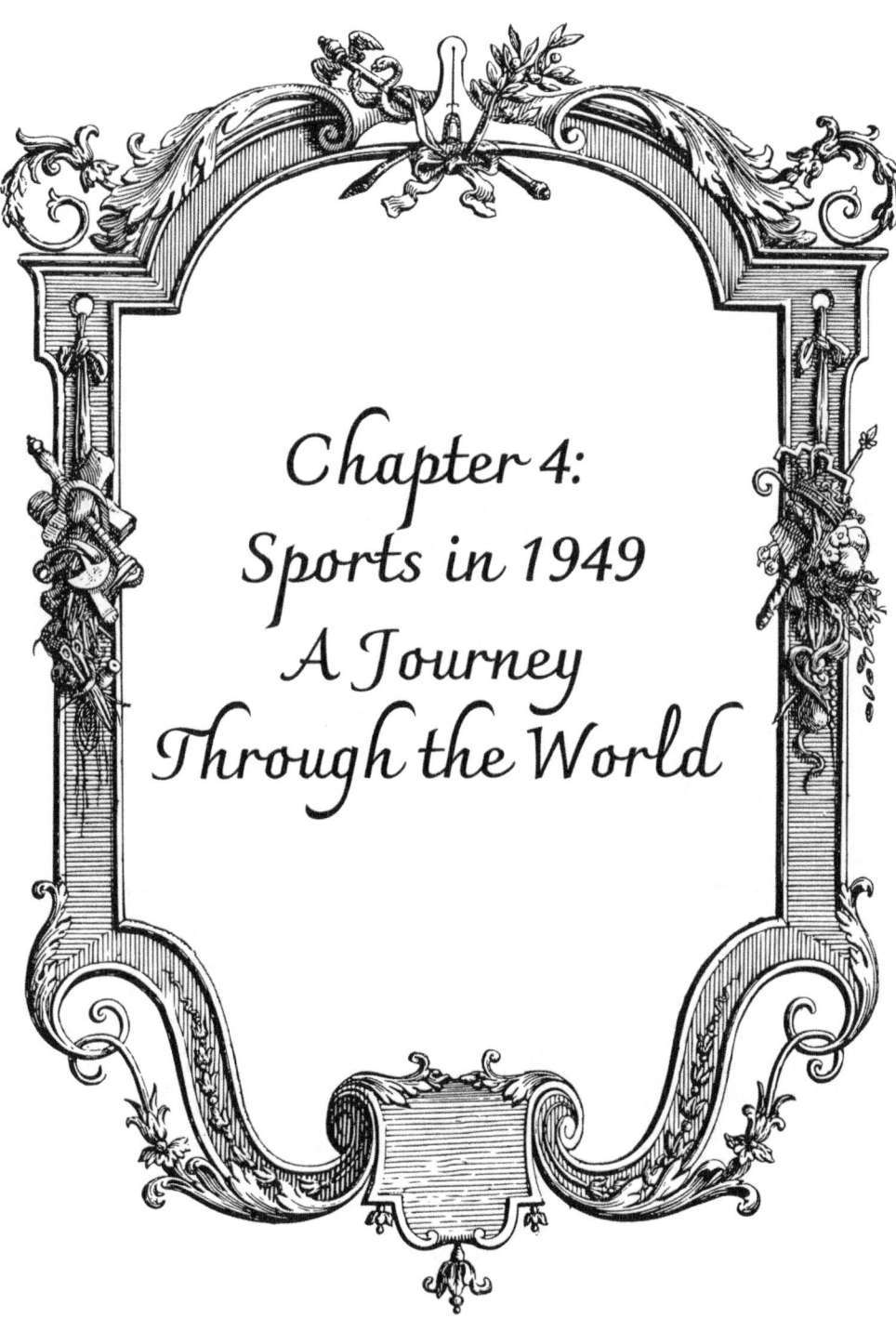

Chapter 4:
Sports in 1949
A Journey
Through the World

Several memorable achievements and victories took place in the world of sports in 1949. Some of the notable events and accomplishments from that year include:

Football

The successes of the Cleveland Browns in the All-America Football Conference (AAFC) and the Philadelphia Eagles in the National Football League (NFL) showcased the prominence of professional American football during this period.

Baseball

Joe DiMaggio's remarkable 56-game hitting streak in Major League Baseball (MLB) garnered widespread attention and remains one of the most significant records in the sport's history.

Boxing

Ezzard Charles defeated Jersey Joe Walcott to become the heavyweight boxing champion, marking a significant moment in the world of professional boxing.

Tennis

Pancho Gonzales won the U.S. National Championships (now known as the U.S. Open) in tennis, showcasing his exceptional skill and dominance on the court.

Golf

Sam Snead won the PGA Championship, solidifying his status as one of the premier golfers of the era and further enhancing his legacy in the sport.

Ice Hockey

The Toronto Maple Leafs' victory in the National Hockey League (NHL) Stanley Cup in 1949 further solidified the team's historical significance and celebrated legacy in the realm of professional ice hockey.

The victory also served to inspire generations of ice hockey enthusiasts in Canada and around the world, contributing to the continued growth and popularity of the sport on a global scale.

Basketball

The Basketball Association of America (BAA) merged with the National Basketball League (NBL) to form the National Basketball Association (NBA), marking a significant moment in the history of professional basketball this year.

Horse Racing

Events such as the Kentucky Derby, the Preakness Stakes, and the Belmont Stakes continued to captivate horse racing enthusiasts, showcasing the talents of various racehorses and jockeys

the Kentucky Derby

Motor Racing

Juan Manuel Fangio, the Argentine racing driver, indeed made a significant impact in the world of motorsports in 1949, laying the foundation for his illustrious career. His triumph in the Formula One World Championship marked the beginning of a series of achievements that solidified his legacy as one of the greatest Formula One drivers of all time.

Activity: Test Your Knowledge of 1949 Sports History

Enjoy the multiple-choice quiz and see how well you remember the exciting sports history of 1949!

1. Which team dominated the All-America Football Conference (AAFC) in 1949, winning their fourth consecutive championship?
a) San Francisco 49ers
b) New York Yankees
c) Cleveland Browns
d) Chicago Bears

2. In 1949, which baseball legend achieved a remarkable 56-game hitting streak, a record that still stands today?
a) Mickey Mantle
b) Ted Williams
c) Joe DiMaggio
d) Jackie Robinson

3. Who did Ezzard Charles defeat to become the heavyweight boxing champion in 1949?
a) Joe Louis
b) Rocky Marciano
c) Jersey Joe Walcott
d) Max Baer

4. In 1949, which golfer secured the PGA Championship, adding to his impressive list of achievements in the world of golf?
a) Ben Hogan
b) Byron Nelson
c) Bobby Jones
d) Sam Snead

5. Which team clinched the National Hockey League (NHL) Stanley Cup in 1949, solidifying their place in hockey history?
a) Detroit Red Wings
b) Toronto Maple Leafs
c) Montreal Canadiens
d) Boston Bruins

6. Which Argentine racing driver made a significant impact in the world of motorsports in 1949, showcasing exceptional skills and determination?
a) Juan Manuel Fangio
b) José Froilán González
c) Carlos Reutemann
d) Oscar Gálvez

7. Who won the National League MVP award in Major League Baseball (MLB) for his outstanding performance in the 1949 season?
a) Jackie Robinson
b) Stan Musial
c) Roy Campanella
d) Ralph Kiner

8. In 1949, which football team claimed victory in the Rose Bowl, cementing their position as one of the top college football teams of the year?
a) Notre Dame Fighting Irish
b) Michigan Wolverines
c) USC Trojans
d) Ohio State Buckeyes

Chapter 5: Fashion, and Popular Leisure Activities

Fashion

Fashion and popular leisure activities in 1949 were influenced by the post-World War II era and the subsequent emergence of a new cultural landscape. Some notable trends and activities from that time:

Women's fashion

New Silhouettes

Women's fashion in 1949 embraced a more feminine and glamorous aesthetic. The hourglass silhouette, with its nipped-in waist and full skirts, became increasingly popular, emphasizing a woman's curves and highlighting a more graceful and elegant appearance.

Accessories

Accessories played a significant role in complementing women's fashion in 1949. Here are some of the popular accessories that were in vogue during that time:

Hats: Women commonly wore a variety of hats to add flair to their outfits. These included wide-brimmed hats, pillbox hats, and small, intricate headpieces adorned with feathers, flowers, or ribbons.

Gloves: Gloves were a staple accessory for women's fashion in the 1940s. Elbow-length gloves made from silk, satin, or cotton were particularly fashionable and were often worn with more formal attire.

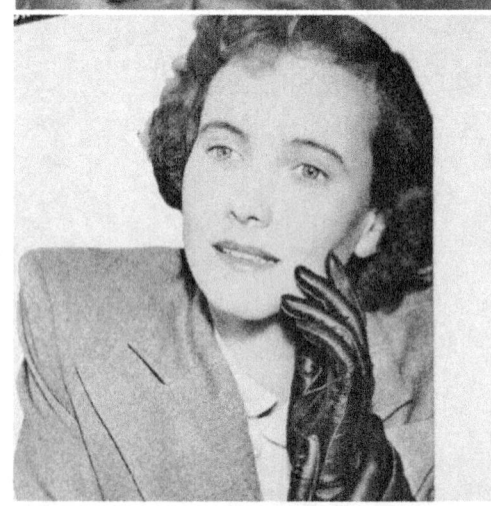

Handbags: Structured handbags with short handles were popular. Box-shaped purses made of leather or fabric, often featuring simple designs or embellishments, were commonly carried to complement the overall look.

Accessories

Scarves: Scarves were used to add a touch of elegance to outfits. Silk scarves in vibrant colors or with intricate patterns were often tied around the neck or worn as a headscarf.

Shoes: Women's shoes in 1949 were often heeled and stylish. Peep-toe pumps, wedge heels, and slingbacks were fashionable choices. Two-tone shoes, often in a combination of white and another color, were also popular.

Belts: Wide, cinched belts were commonly worn to emphasize the waistline and complement the feminine silhouette. They were often made from leather and featured decorative buckles or intricate detailing.

Jewelry: Costume jewelry and statement pieces were essential in completing the 1949 look. Pearls, brooches, and large, bold necklaces were particularly popular. Earrings, often in the form of chandelier or hoop styles, were also commonly worn.

Hairstyles

Hairstyles for women in 1949 emphasized elegance and femininity, with popular choices including victory rolls, short curls, and the classic pageboy haircut. Glamorous waves and the chignon updo also gained traction

Fashion for Men in 1949
Tailored Suits

Men's fashion in 1949 favored well-tailored suits with broad shoulders and a more relaxed fit. The silhouette was often characterized by a single-breasted, two-button jacket, and high-waisted trousers, contributing to a polished and distinguished appearance.

Accessories

Accessories for men included ties, fedora hats, and polished dress shoes, contributing to a well-groomed and sophisticated appearance. These elements added a touch of refinement and completed the overall look for both formal and casual attire.

Popular Leisure Activities

Besides the entertainment activities mentioned, leisure activities provided people with ways to relax, socialize, and enjoy their free time during the post-World War II era.

Outdoor Activities

Engaging in outdoor activities like hiking and picnicking, were popular ways for individuals to stay active and enjoy nature.

Board Games and Puzzles

Families and friends often spent time together playing board games and solving puzzles, fostering a sense of camaraderie and friendly competition within the household.

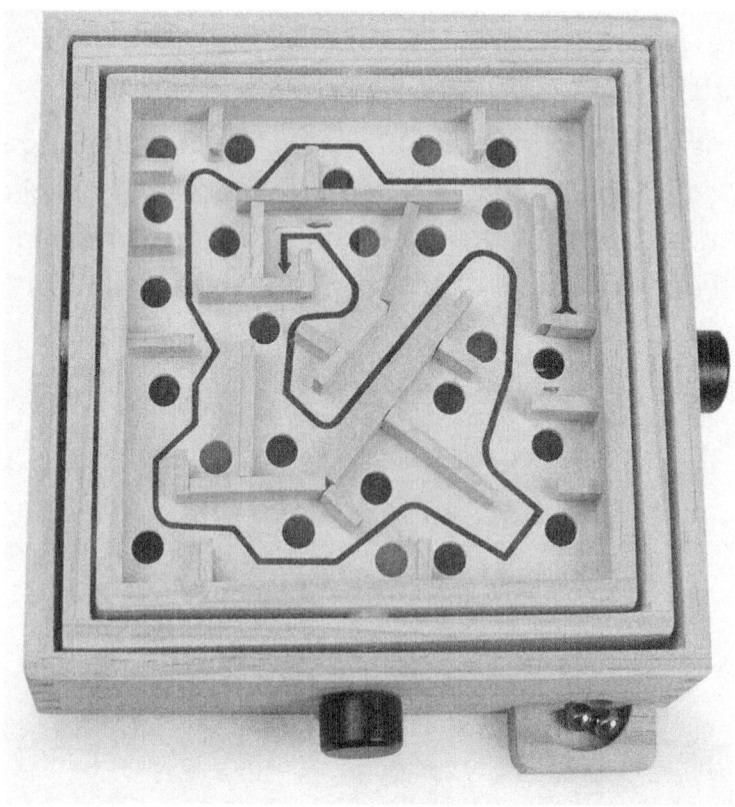

Activity: Let's draw a picture of "fashion of 1949"

Enjoy your artistic exploration of the fashion of 1949!

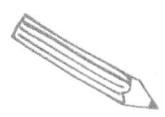

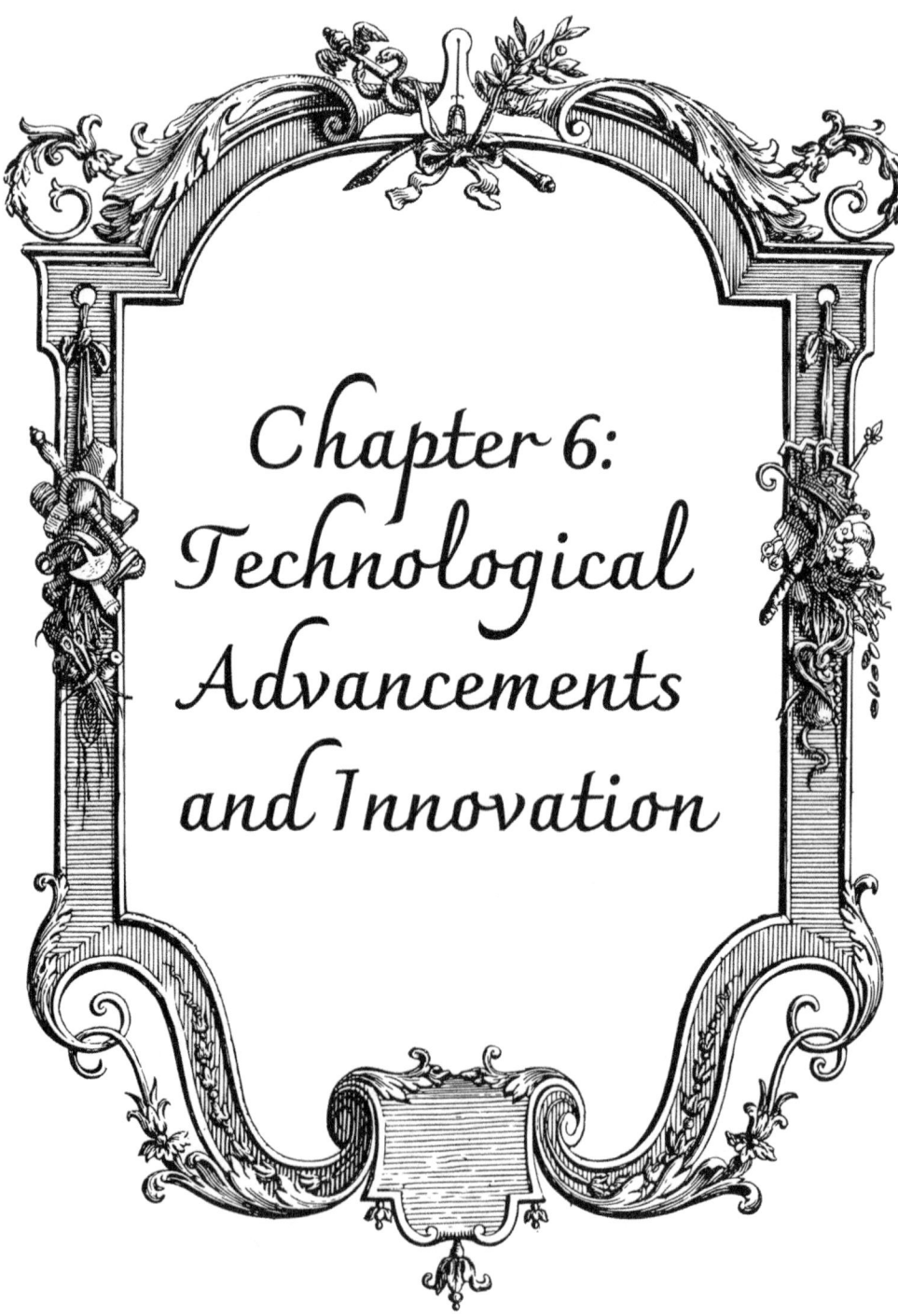

Chapter 6: Technological Advancements and Innovation

Technological events

In 1949, several significant technological advancements and inventions were made, shaping the course of modern technology and its applications. Some of the notable technological achievements and inventions during this period include:

The first automatic street lights

The installation of the first automatic street lights in New Milford, Connecticut in 1949 marked a notable advancement in urban infrastructure and technology. Automatic street lights, equipped with light sensors or timers, offered improved efficiency and convenience compared to traditional manual street lighting systems.

The successful adoption of automatic street lights in New Milford served as a model for other cities and communities, leading to widespread adoption of similar technologies worldwide

45 rpm Record USA

The 45 rpm record, a type of phonograph record format, was introduced in the United States, revolutionizing the music industry and setting a new standard for audio recording and playback.

The Ferranti Mark 1, the world's first commercially available computer, was released, signifying a monumental leap in computing technology and laying the groundwork for the development of modern computers and information systems.

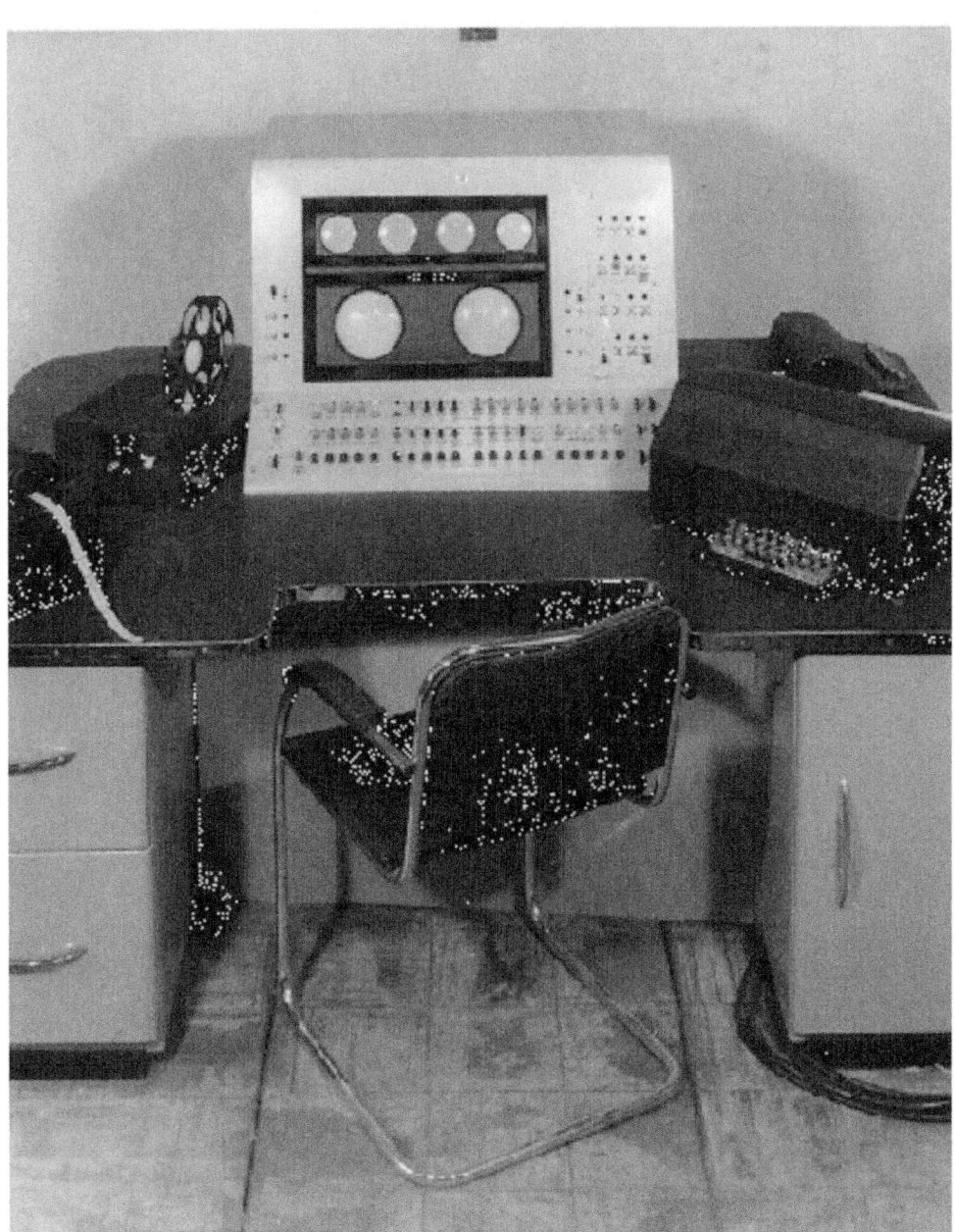

The world's first helicopter by Igor Sikorsky

The De Havilland Comet, the world's first commercial passenger jet airliner, conducted its inaugural test flight on July 27, 1949. Designed and produced by De Havilland in Hertfordshire, England, the Comet marked a groundbreaking advancement in the field of commercial aviation.

The Comet remained in production in various forms until the late 1990s, leaving an enduring legacy in the annals of aviation history as the pioneer of modern commercial jet travel.

The Automobiles of 1949

In 1949, the automotive industry was undergoing a significant transformation, as the effects of World War II were starting to fade, and various car manufacturers were focusing on innovation and design to cater to the growing demands of consumers.

- **1949 Ford**

The 1949 Ford is often seen as a symbol of the post-war American dream, representing a blend of style, performance, and affordability that captured the spirit of the time. Its impact on automotive design and engineering cemented its place in history as an iconic and influential vehicle.

- **Rolls-Royce Silver Dawn**

The Rolls-Royce Silver Dawn is a luxury car that was produced by Rolls-Royce Limited. It remains an important part of the company's history, representing a period of transition and adaptation for one of the world's most renowned luxury car manufacturers.

- **Borgward Hansa 1500**

The Borgward Hansa 1500 is a medium-sized automobile manufactured by the Bremen. It was first presented at the Geneva Motor Show in March 1949 [4] and production commenced on 13 October 1949. It is often seen as the first all new model launched by the German auto industry after the <u>war</u>

- **Austin A90 Atlantic**

The Austin A90 Atlantic was a British car produced by the Austin Motor Company in 1949. It was a luxury car that aimed to cater to the upper end of the market and was designed to target the North American market, particularly the United States. It represents an important chapter in the history of the Austin Motor Company and the British automotive industry as a whole.

- **Oldsmobile 88**

The Oldsmobile 88 remains a celebrated classic car among enthusiasts and collectors, appreciated for its historical significance, innovative engineering, and its role in shaping the American automotive landscape.

Activity: Test Your Knowledge of Technology in 1949

Enjoy some fill-in-the-blank questions related to the technological advancements and innovations in 1949

1. The introduction of the ___ in the United States revolutionized the music industry, allowing for the more efficient production and distribution of music.

2. ___ is credited with the creation of the world's first helicopter in 1949, marking a significant milestone in the history of aviation.

3. The automobile models of 1949 showcased several innovative features, including streamlined designs, improved ___ efficiency, and advanced safety technologies.

4. The installation of the first automatic street lights in ___ marked a notable advancement in urban infrastructure and technology

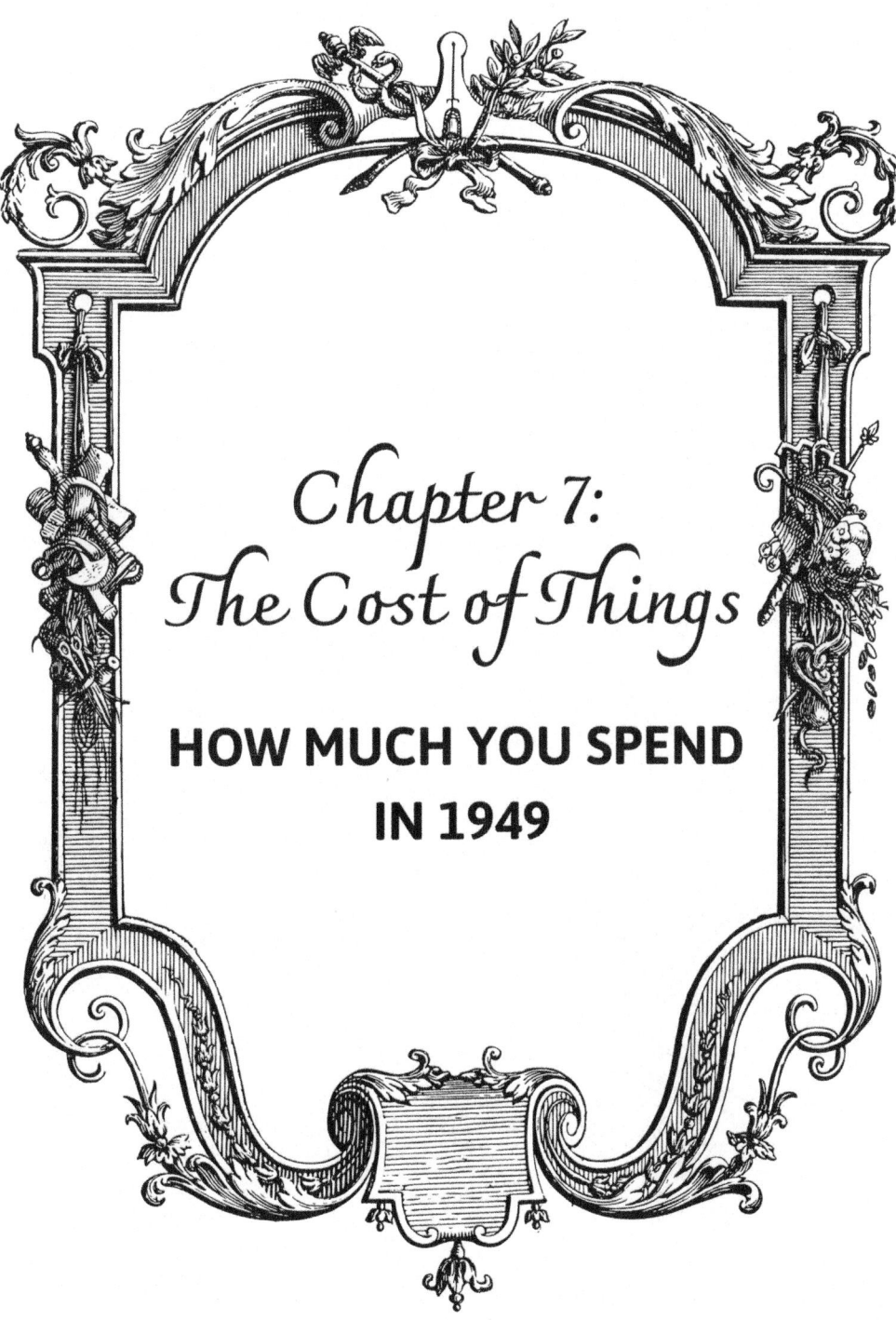

Chapter 7: The Cost of Things

HOW MUCH YOU SPEND IN 1949

Cost of Living in 1949

The cost of living in 1949 was significantly different compared to present times. While specific prices may vary depending on the location and various other factors, some general information about the cost of living during this year:

- *Average Cost of new house $7,450.00*
- *Average wages per year $2,950.00*
- *Minimum Hourly Wage Rate 70 cents per hour*

Cost of Living in 1949

- Cost of a gallon of Gas 17 cents
- Average Cost New Car $1,420.00

Cost of Living in 1949

Food

- Bread: 14 cents/loaf
- Milk: 84 cents/gal
- Bacon per pound 50 cents
- Dobbs Hat $8.50
- Kitchen Table and Chairs $100.00
- Bacon Sliced 59 cents per pound
- Bananas 11 cents per pound
- Bleach 21 cents 1/2 gallon
- Cantaloupe 23 cents
- Coffee 85 cents for 2 pound bag
- Fresh Chickens 55 cents per pound

Activity: How the life changed

Comparing prices from 1949 with the cost of similar items in the present day. Reflect on the changes in consumer behavior

Chapter 8: Births in 1949

Several notable individuals were born in 1949 across various fields, including politics, entertainment, and sports. Some famous births from that year:

1. Andy Kaufman

Andy Kaufman, born on January 17, 1949, in New York City, New York, was indeed a unique and unconventional comedian known for his boundary-pushing and avant-garde performances. He was celebrated for his eccentric and often controversial acts, which challenged traditional notions of comedy and performance art.
Kaufman's innovative and boundary-pushing approach to comedy continues to influence comedians and performance artists to this day, cementing his legacy as a trailblazer in the world of alternative comedy and performance art.

2. John Belushi

John Belushi, born on February 4, 1949, in Chicago, Illinois, was indeed a prominent American comedian and actor known for his dynamic and energetic performances. He gained widespread recognition for his work on the sketch comedy show "Saturday Night Live". One of his most famous roles was as "Joliet" Jake Blues in the cult classic film "The Blues Brothers,". His contributions to comedy and entertainment continue to be remembered and celebrated, solidifying his legacy as one of the most influential and beloved comedians of his time.

3. Patrick Duffy

Patrick Duffy, born on March 17, 1949, in Townsend, Montana, is a well-known American actor, recognized for his notable roles in popular television series. He gained widespread fame for his portrayal of Bobby Ewing in the long-running television drama "Dallas," Following his success on "Dallas," Duffy went on to star in the family sitcom "Step by Step," which aired from 1991 to 1998.

His contributions to the entertainment industry have earned him a dedicated fan base and a lasting place in the history of American television.

4. Vera Wang

Vera Wang, born on June 27, 1949, in New York City, is indeed a highly influential American fashion designer renowned for her exquisite bridal gowns and high-end couture collections. Wang first gained recognition in the fashion industry as a prominent figure in the world of upscale bridal wear, and her designs quickly became synonymous with sophistication, elegance, and modern luxury.

Over the years, her position is as a prominent and influential figure in the global fashion industry.

5. Lionel Richie

Lionel Richie, born on June 20, 1949, in Tuskegee, Alabama, is a highly acclaimed American singer, songwriter, and producer, known for his immense contributions to the music industry. Richie gained prominence as a member of the soul and R&B group Commodores before embarking on a successful solo career. As the lead vocalist for the Commodores, Richie contributed to the group's success with hits such as "Easy" and "Three Times a Lady."

His enduring influence and contributions to the music industry have earned him numerous accolades, including Grammy Awards and the praise of both fans and peers alike, solidifying his legacy as one of the most celebrated musicians of his generation.

6. Gloria Gaynor

Gloria Gaynor, born on September 7, 1949, in Newark, New Jersey, is a renowned American singer known for her influential contributions to the disco and dance music genres. She rose to international fame in the late 1970s with her iconic hit song "I Will Survive," which has since become an enduring anthem of empowerment and resilience.

In addition to "I Will Survive," Gloria Gaynor has released numerous other successful songs, contributing to her lasting impact on the music world. Her music often combines elements of disco, pop, and soul, and her dynamic performances have earned her a dedicated fan base and critical acclaim. Gaynor's legacy as a pioneering figure in the disco era and her enduring influence on popular music have secured her a special place in the history of American music.

7. Bruce Springsteen

Bruce Springsteen, born on September 23, 1949, in Long Branch, New Jersey, is indeed a celebrated American singer, songwriter, and musician, known for his profound influence on rock music and American culture. Springsteen is often referred to as "The Boss," a nickname that reflects his commanding stage presence and his ability to connect with audiences through his powerful and heartfelt performances.

Springsteen first gained widespread acclaim in the 1970s with his E Street Band, and his poetic lyrics and passionate performances quickly established him as a prominent figure in the rock music scene. His album "Born to Run," released in 1975, solidified his status as a rock icon, and subsequent albums such as "Darkness on the Edge of Town" and "Born in the U.S.A." further cemented his reputation as a leading voice in American rock music and resonated with audiences worldwide.

8. Sigourney Weaver

Sigourney Weaver, born on October 8, 1949, in Manhattan, New York, is an acclaimed American actress known for her versatile performances and her contributions to the science fiction and action film genres. She gained widespread recognition and critical acclaim for her iconic role as Ellen Ripley in the "Alien" film series. She has starred in notable movies such as "Ghostbusters," "Gorillas in the Mist," "Working Girl," and "Avatar,"

Weaver's contributions to the film industry have earned her numerous accolades, including Academy Award nominations, and she remains a respected and influential figure in the world of cinema.

9. Jeff Bridges

Born on December 4, Jeff Bridges, is indeed an acclaimed American actor known for his versatility and memorable performances in a wide range of films. He has starred in numerous acclaimed films, including "The Last Picture Show," "Tron," "Starman," "The Fabulous Baker Boys," and "True Grit," among others. However, perhaps one of his most iconic and beloved roles is that of Jeff "The Dude" Lebowski in the cult classic film "The Big Lebowski,"His performance in "Crazy Heart" earned him widespread acclaim and accolades, including an Academy Award for Best Actor,

His commitment to his craft and his ability to embody a diverse array of characters have solidified his status as one of the most respected and talented actors in Hollywood.

10. Maurice Gibb

Maurice Gibb, born on December 22, 1949, on the Isle of Man, was indeed a prominent musician and a member of the highly successful British pop band the Bee Gees. Maurice played a significant role in the group's success and contributed to their enduring legacy in the music industry. In addition to his work with the Bee Gees, Maurice Gibb was also a talented multi-instrumentalist and songwriter, contributing to the band's songwriting and musical arrangements. His contributions to popular music have left a lasting impact on the music industry and continue to be celebrated by fans and music enthusiasts globally.

Activity: "Profiles in Achievement: The Noteworthy Births of 1949"

1. Who was born on January 17, 1949, and known for his eccentric and unconventional comedy performances, often blurring the lines between reality and performance art?
a) Patrick Duffy
b) Andy Kaufman
c) Jeff Bridges
d) Vera Wang

2. Who is the American actor known for his roles in the TV series "Dallas" and "Step by Step"?
a) Gloria Gaynor
b) Bruce Springsteen
c) Patrick Duffy
d) Andy Kaufman

3. Born on June 27, 1949, who is the prominent American fashion designer known for her elegant and sophisticated bridal gowns and haute couture collections?
a) Vera Wang
b) Jeff Bridges
c) Maurice Gibb
d) Lionel Richie

4. When was Gloria Gaynor born?

a) March 17, 1949

b) June 20, 1949

c) September 7, 1949

d) December 22, 1949

5. When was Lionel Richie born?

a) September 7, 1949

b) June 20, 1949

c) September 23, 1949

d) December 4, 1949

6. Born on February 4, 1949, which American comedian and actor gained fame for his work on "Saturday Night Live" and in films like "The Blues Brothers"?

a) Maurice Gibb

b) Lionel Richie

c) John Belushi

d) Sigourney Weaver

7. When was Bruce Springsteen born?

a) March 17, 1949

b) June 20, 1949

c) September 23, 1949

d) December 4, 1949

8. Born on October 8, 1949, which American actress is known for her roles in iconic films such as the "Alien" series and "Avatar"?

a) John Belushi

b) Sigourney Weaver

c) Lionel Richie

d) Andy Kaufman

9. Born on December 4, 1949, who is the acclaimed American actor known for his roles in films such as "The Big Lebowski" and "Crazy Heart"?

a) Vera Wang

b) Gloria Gaynor

c) Jeff Bridges

d) Patrick Duffy

10. Which member of the Bee Gees made significant contributions to the band's success?

a) Maurice Gibb

b) Bruce Springsteen

c) Sigourney Weaver

d) John Belushi

Do you know Celebrities Born in 1949?

We have heartfelt thank-you gifts for you

As a token of our appreciation for joining us on this historical journey through 1949, we've included a set of cards and stamps inspired by the year of 1949. These cards are your canvas to capture the essence of the past. We encourage you to use them as inspiration for creating your own unique cards, sharing your perspective on the historical moments we've explored in this book. Whether it's a holiday greeting or a simple hello to a loved one, these cards are your way to connect with the history we've uncovered together.

Happy creating!

Activity answers

Chapter 1

1. d) Council of Europe
2. c) Mao Zedong
3. b) Jawaharlal Nehru
4. b) Joseph Stalin
5. c) Harry S. Truman
6. b) Shigeru Yoshida
7. b) Military alliance against the Soviet Union
8. b) Alcide De Gasperi

Chapter 2

1. Riders in the Sky
2. Some Enchanted Evening
3. That Lucky Old Sun
4. Slippin' Around

Chapter 3

Chapter 4:
1. c) Cleveland Browns
2. c) Joe DiMaggio
3. c) Jersey Joe Walcott
4. d) Sam Snead
5. b) Toronto Maple Leafs
6. a) Juan Manuel Fangio
7. a) Jackie Robinson
8. c) USC Trojans

Chapter 6:
1. 45 rpm record
2. Igor Sikorsky
3. fuel
4. New Milford, Connecticut

Chapter 8:
1. b) Andy Kaufman
2. c) Patrick Duffy
3. a) Vera Wang
4. c) September 7, 1949
5. b) June 20, 1949
6. c) John Belushi
7. c) September 23, 1949
8. b) Sigourney Weaver
9. c) Jeff Bridges
10. a) Maurice Gibb

Embracing 1949: A Grateful Farewell

Celebrating 1949: A Voyage Through History

Join us in honoring the remarkable spirit of 1949, a year filled with stories of resilience and progress. Let's explore the moments that defined this era and discover the lasting impact it has had on our world.

Preserve the Memories, Share the Journey

Your participation has enriched our understanding of the events that unfolded in 1949. Your insights and reflections are invaluable in ensuring that the essence of this pivotal year remains alive. Together, let's cherish the legacy of '49 and safeguard its significance for generations to come.
Until then, thank you for being part of our cherished journey.

Copyright © Edward Art Lab 2023

All rights reserved. No part of this publication may be reproduced, distributed, or transmitted in any form or by any means, including photocopying, recording, or other electronic or mechanical methods, without the prior written permission of the publisher, except in the case of brief quotations embodied in critical reviews and certain other noncommercial uses permitted by copyright law.

Happy Birthday
note

HAPPY BIRTHDAY NOTE

TO DO LIST

Name: _____ Day: _____ Month: _____

No	To Do List	Yes	No

TO DO LIST

Name: _____ Day: _____ Month: _____

No	To Do List	Yes	No

TO DO LIST

Name: _____   Day: _____   Month: _____

No	To Do List	Yes	No

NOTE

NOTE

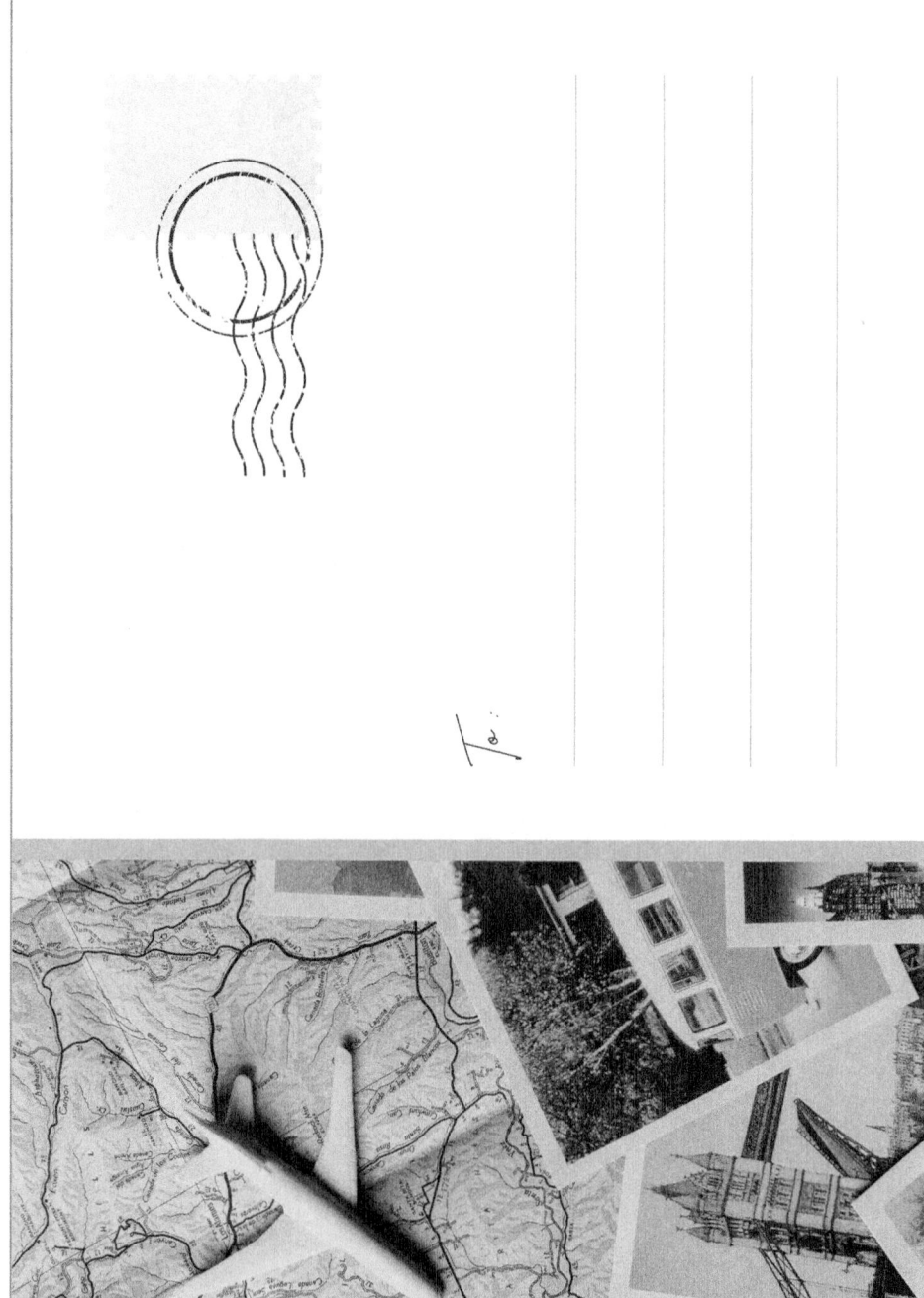

Remember This!

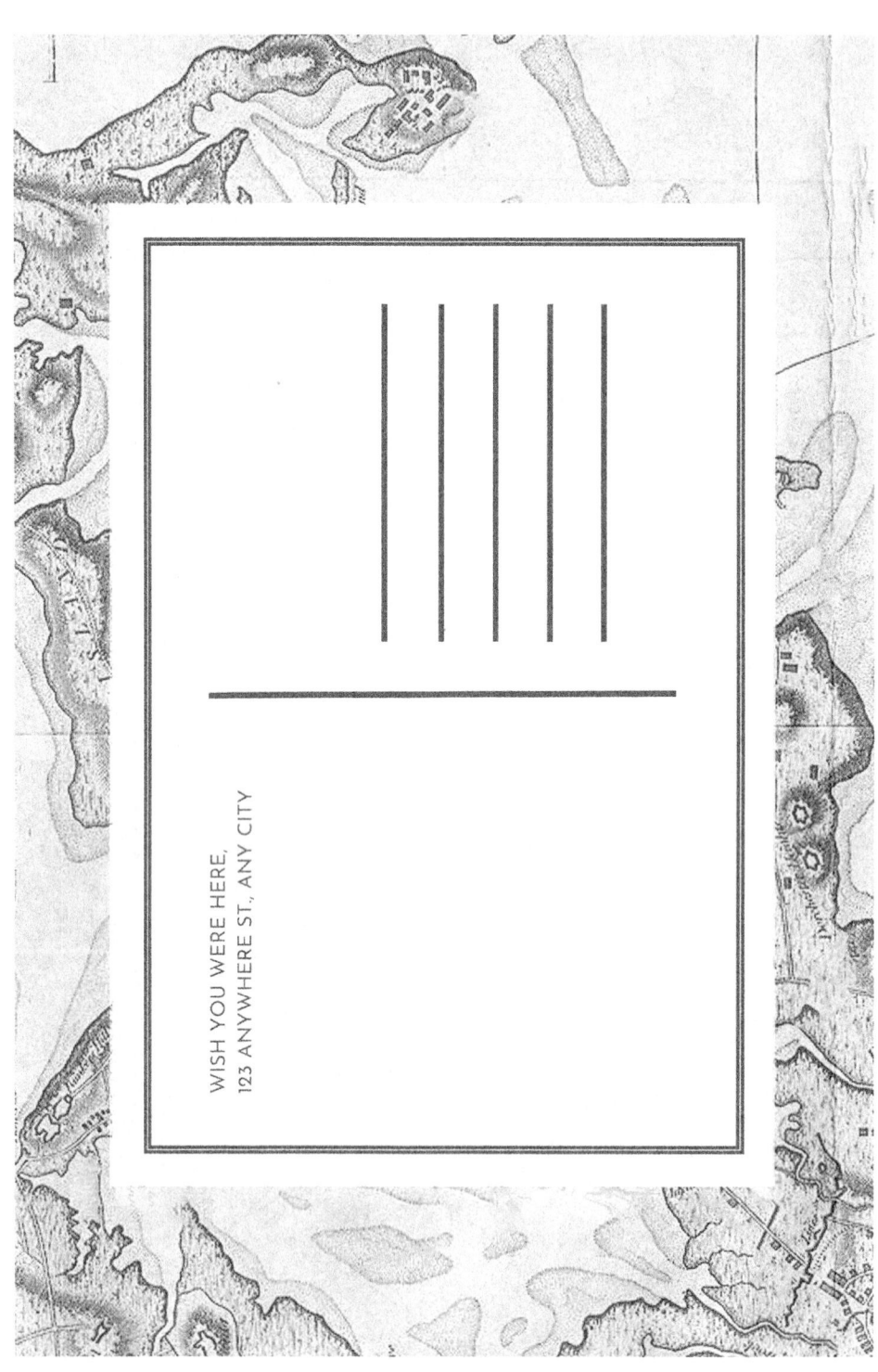

Printed in Great Britain
by Amazon